ROYAL ESCAPE

ROYAL ESCAPE

By Charles Buchanan

Illustrated by Stephen Millingen

ANGLIA *young* BOOKS

First published in 1994
by Anglia Young Books
Durhams Farmhouse
Ickleton
Saffron Walden, Essex CB10 1SR

© 1994 Charles Buchanan

All rights reserved. No part of this publication may be reproduced, stored in a retrieval system, or transmitted in any form or by any means, electronic, mechanical, photocopying, recording or otherwise without the written permission of the Publisher.

Illustrations by Stephen Millingen

British Library Cataloguing-in-Publication Data

A catalogue record for this book is available from the British Library

ISBN 1 871173 40 X

Typeset in Palatino and printed in Great Britain by
Redwood Books, Trowbridge, Wilts

AUTHOR'S NOTE

In 1625 Charles I became King of England. He believed that he had been chosen to rule the country by God and that he did not have to listen to the advice of Parliament. The quarrels between the King and Parliament eventually led to civil war. Those who fought for the King were known as Cavaliers and Parliament's soldiers were called Roundheads. The leader of the Roundheads was called Oliver Cromwell.

The civil war was won by Parliament and King Charles was put on trial. He was found guilty of causing the war and sentenced to death. He was beheaded in January 1649. To the Cavaliers, the dead King's son was now King Charles II. To try and regain the throne, the young king raised an army to fight the Roundheads. His Cavaliers were beaten at the battle of Dunbar in 1650 but they quickly raised another army mostly made up of Scottish soldiers. On September 3rd 1651, King Charles II personally led his men into battle against the Roundheads. The fighting took place in and around the city of Worcester. The Cavaliers lost the battle and Oliver Cromwell became Lord Protector of England.

The escape of Charles II from the battle of Worcester is well documented. Charles himself told many conflicting accounts to his courtiers after his restoration.

The character of Will Symons is fictional, although the events told in the book are based on documentary evidence. The author has tried to keep the story simple and easy for children to follow. Therefore, many people who were involved in the King's escape have been omitted.

CHAPTER ONE

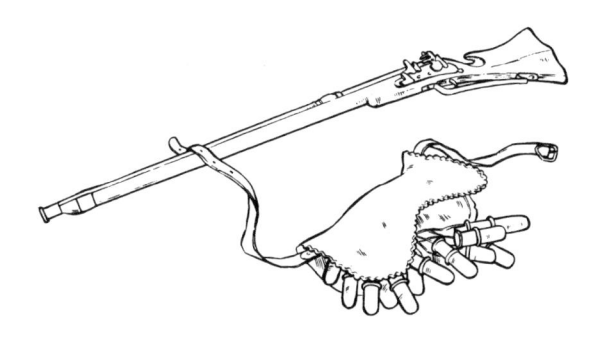

Will Symons held his father's head on his lap. Tears ran down the boy's cheeks.

'Please, Father, don't give up. I'll find a doctor. You'll get better. You must!'

'I'm sorry, Will. I've let you down.'

'Don't say that!' said Will.

'Listen, Son, I haven't much time. You must get away from here. The battle is lost. Try and find your Aunt Martha in Bristol, she'll look after you.'

'I'm not leaving you, Father! I'd rather die here.' Will tried to pick up his father's musket which lay on the ground. It was very heavy. Will dropped it.

'Do as I say, Will. You are the last of my sons.'

'But, I can't just leave you,' Will sobbed.

'You must,' said his father. 'My pain will soon end.

I have done my duty to my King and now you must do yours. Please obey your father's last wish. Go and live!'

John Symons struggled to sit up. Will could see the pain in his father's eyes and he knew that he was dying. John Symons kissed his son on the forehead. 'Remember, I'll always be with you in here.'

John Symons touched his son's heart then his hand fell to the ground.

Will held onto his father and rocked him to and fro. All around him there was musket and cannon fire. The line of Royalist musketeers defending the city walls, was being overrun by the enemy. Men were throwing down their arms and running past him to make their escape in the narrow streets of Worcester, but Will heard and saw nothing. He just sat there, his father's words ringing in his ears. 'You are the last of my sons. Go and live!'

At last Will snapped out of his trance. Gently he laid his father on the ground then he stood looking down at him. He seemed so peaceful. 'He really is at rest,' Will thought.

After a final look at his dead father, Will turned and picked up the fallen musket. But it wasn't made for an eleven year old boy to carry.

At that moment, a cannon ball whistled past his head and Will immediately dropped the musket and ran off down a side street. He took shelter behind the big wooden doors of a stable belonging to an inn. Peering out between the cracks, Will could see Roundhead soldiers going from house to house, shouting, and kicking in the doors. Will thought that they must be looking for Royalist officers, perhaps even for the King himself, if he wasn't already dead. The last sight Will had had of the young King Charles II was about two hours earlier when the King personally led an attack outside the city. Will's father had taken part in it, only to return, badly wounded from a musket ball in the stomach.

Will decided he would stay in the stable until it was dark. Then he would sneak out of the city and make his way south towards Bristol and his Aunt Martha, who was housekeeper for a Royalist family. All he had to do, he told himself, was to keep out of the Roundhead soldiers' way.

Suddenly, Will was seized from behind. A large hand pushed against his mouth.

'Don't shout out!' said the voice of a man. 'I won't harm you. Promise me you won't shout out.'

Will nodded. The hand was taken away and Will's shoulders were turned so that he faced his attacker. The man was very tall and a Royalist officer, of that Will was sure. Even though the man's clothes were dirty and ripped, Oliver Cromwell's officers would never be dressed in such finery.

'Who do you serve, boy?' the man demanded. 'The

rightful King of England or that foul murderer, Oliver Cromwell?'

'I would gladly give my life for King Charles, sir.' said Will.

'Then may God protect you on this evil day.'

'So the battle is lost, Sir?' said Will.

'Aye, lad. The battle is lost.'

'And the King?' said Will.

'On the run. His Royal Majesty is the fox and Cromwell's soldiers are the hounds.' The young man laughed.

'You dare to laugh at the King's troubles?' said Will, shocked and angry.

The man looked more closely at Will. 'You've got spirit,' he said, 'I'll give you that!' Then he went on, more gently. 'Believe me lad, the King himself might laugh. After all, he has set his own hounds on many a fox.'

The man pulled the stable doors slightly ajar and popped his head out. Closing the doors again, he said to Will.

'Can you saddle a horse?' Will nodded. 'I want to get my things from the inn. Saddle the best looking horse in here and have it waiting at the back for me when I come out. I'll only be a couple of minutes. You'll be doing the King and me a big favour.'

'Do you know the King?' said Will, his eyes lighting up.

'Aye, lad, I do. In fact it was His Majesty who sent me here. The horse is for his escape.'

'Then, I will not let you down, Sir.' said Will.

As the tall man prepared to go, he looked hard at Will again.

'I'm taking a great risk. The life of the King of England is in your hands, lad. How do I know I can trust you?'

'Because my four brothers, and now my father, have all died fighting for King Charles.'

The man could see the tears in Will's eyes. He put his hand on the boy's shoulder.

When the man had left, Will picked out a chestnut mare from the four horses in the stable and saddled her. He then made sure there were no Roundhead soldiers outside before leading the mare into the courtyard at the back of the inn. There he waited.

Suddenly, from inside the inn, Will heard a lot of banging and shouting. He looked up and saw the back door on the upper storey burst open. Two men fell out onto the wooden balcony. They were locked together in a desperate struggle. One of them, Will saw, was the tall man, the other was a Roundhead soldier. They picked themselves up and the Roundhead lunged at the tall man with a dagger, but the tall man side stepped and then headbutted the soldier in the stomach. At the same moment he pushed the groaning soldier over the balcony rail. The Roundhead would have fallen on Will and the mare if the boy hadn't pulled the horse out of the way.

'Well done, lad!' called down the man, laughing.

'Watch out!' Will shouted up at the balcony.

He had seen another soldier come up behind the tall man. But his warning came too late. The soldier hit him on the back of the head with the butt of his musket. The tall man fell over the balcony and landed on top of the first soldier.

'Are you all right?' said Will. 'Can you stand?'

'Yes, I think so. Quickly, lad, help me get on the horse.'

Will helped the man to his feet. He was still a little groggy. As he was putting the man's foot into a stirrup, Will looked up and saw to his horror that the Roundhead soldier on the balcony was about to fire his musket. Without thinking, Will picked up a large stone and threw it upwards with all his might. It struck the soldier just under his helmet,

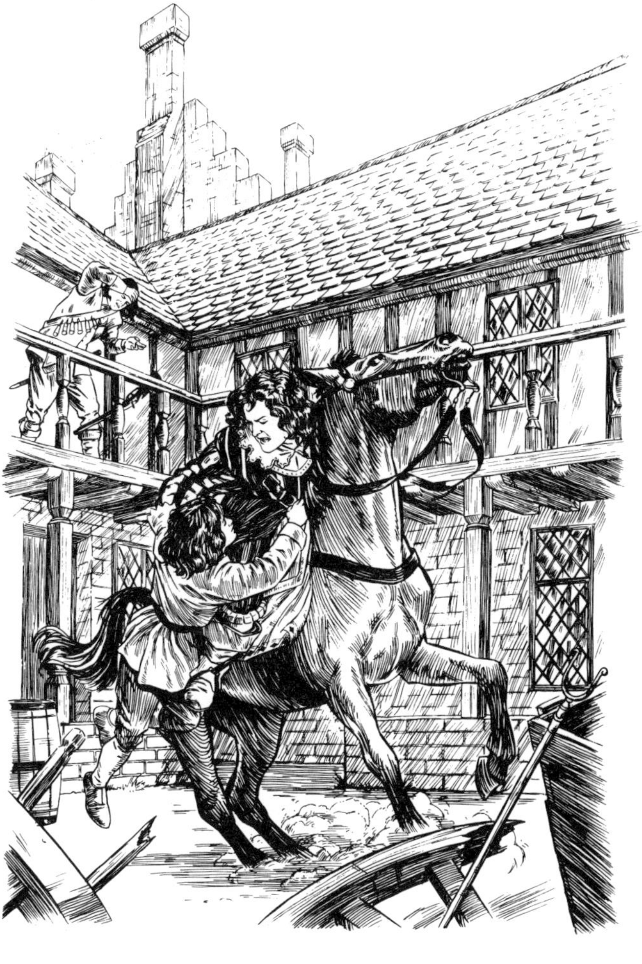

right in the middle of his forehead. He yelled in pain and dropped his musket.

The man, now safely in the saddle, held out his hand to Will.

'Come on, lad, take hold! Hurry, there is no time to lose!'

Will obeyed and immediately scrambled up behind.

A voice cried out from above.

'Charles Stuart, so called 'King of England', I arrest you in the name of Parliament!'

Will couldn't believe his ears.

'You're the King!' he said, wide eyed.

'That I am, lad! And thanks to you, I'm still alive. Now put your arms around my waist and hold on tight. And keep your head down!'

CHAPTER TWO

The King skilfully turned the chestnut mare around and galloped out of the yard. Will heard two muskets fire and felt the balls whistle past either side of his head. In the street, a small group of patrolling Roundhead soldiers were taken by surprise. The King rode straight through them, sending them sprawling to the ground. More musket fire was aimed at the fleeing riders. Will shut his eyes and hung on to Charles's waist. When he opened them again, they were passing through St Martin's Gate which led north, out of Worcester, and towards open countryside.

Charles gave his mare no rest. As they rode, they passed many of the fleeing Scottish soldiers who had fought on the King's side. They were making their way home, which was still more than 200 miles away.

Will called out to the King. 'Your Majesty, if you don't slow down, this mare will drop down dead.'

'Aye, lad, I know you're right' said Charles, turning his head slightly so that Will could hear him. 'But, I must catch up with my senior officers.'

'Well if you don't find them soon, we'll be *running* after them.'

Charles smiled to himself. Never in his life had anyone been so blunt with him, not even his generals, and here was a young peasant boy telling him how stupid he was being. He found the experience quite refreshing.

A few minutes later, the King caught sight of a large group of Royalist horsemen, or Cavaliers as they were known, up ahead. They were bunched together in the middle of the road. As he and Will approached them, they heard loud angry voices.

'We must continue north to Scotland, it is our only hope,' said one Cavalier.

'No,' said another, 'we must wait until we get news of the King.'

'Well said, Sir, but your wait is already over.'

The arguing men looked at Charles in astonishment. Then they all jumped off their horses, and knelt on the ground.

'Your Majesty!' they cried.

'Gentlemen, it is good to see that so many of you

survived the battle. Now, let me introduce to you a young friend of mine, Will Symons.' Charles turned slightly in the saddle so that the kneeling nobility could look up and see Will, the son of a peasant. 'Wherever I go,' continued Charles, 'Will shall go with me.'

Soon the Cavaliers were again discussing their next move. Lord Derby, the most important noble man still free, wanted the King to make his way to Scotland. But Charles had other plans.

'The last time I was in Scotland, I was almost a prisoner there. And travelling in large numbers will only attract the attention of our enemies.'

Will could see what the King meant. Hundreds of frightened, weary men were joining the Royal party. There was no way that they could make their escape quietly across country. Charles thought this was rather funny. 'When I wanted them by my side in the battle,' he said, 'they all ran away and left me. Now, I can't seem to get rid of them!'

At last Charles said, 'I think that Will and I should make for London.' Then he turned to his boyhood friend, Lord Wilmot. 'And I want you to come with us Wilmot.'

The first problem, though, was to find shelter that night. Lord Derby suggested they make for a big house called 'Boscobel', which was hidden in a large forest not far away.

'The house is owned by a Mr Giffard, Your Majesty,' said Lord Derby. 'He gave me shelter a few months ago when I was wounded in battle. And, he is a Catholic.'

'Excellent!' said Charles.

'I don't understand,' said Lord Wilmot. "Why is the fact that Mr Giffard is a Catholic so important?'

'Because, My Lord,' said Will, 'his house will have secret hiding places.'

Lord Wilmot frowned at Will. How dare a peasant boy speak to him without being asked? Charles laughed at the expression on his noble friend's face.

'The boy is right, Wilmot. Catholics have to do everything in secret. Our friend, Oliver Cromwell, does not allow them to worship God in their own way. So, their houses are full of hidden rooms where they can hide their priests or other Catholics on the run.'

'But how do we know we can trust Mr Giffard?' said Wilmot.

'Because all Catholics are loyal supporters of the Crown,' said the King. He paused for a moment and looked at Will. Then he said, 'Many have died fighting for me and my father.'

A man whispered in Lord Derby's ear and he

became suddenly excited. 'Your Majesty,' he said, 'one of my men has just informed me that Mr Giffard is with our party. I have sent for him.'

The King nodded and Mr Giffard, together with his servant Francis Yates, were presented to the King. ' I would be honoured to serve His Majesty,' said Mr Giffard.

The royal party was led off the main road road by Francis Yates. Yates was a local man and knew all the quiet tracks and by-roads. They rode all night and saw no Roundhead patrols. At three o' clock in the morning, they stopped at a house near 'Boscobel', which was also owned by Mr Giffard.

'I think Your Majesty will be safer in a smaller house,' said Mr Giffard. 'The tenant here is a man called George Penderel. You will find him a true and honest servant of the Crown.'

George Penderel did not hesitate when Mr Giffard told him that he had the King outside his door. He immediately opened up his house, even though he knew that if Oliver Cromwell's troops found out, he could be shot. He told the King that there was a band of Roundheads only three miles away.

Mr Giffard said, 'Your Majesty must get rid of every single one of your companions.'

After a short meeting, it was decided that King Charles and Will would try and make their escape to London alone, guided by the Penderel family.

Lord Wilmot would also stay in the area, until he was sure that the King had got away, and then would meet up with him in London. Lord Derby was to lead the rest of the men away to join three thousand Scottish troops, who were also close by, who had not taken part in the battle of Worcester. They would then try and make their way back to Scotland.

'Your Majesty will have to get rid of those fine clothes,' said George Penderel, once Lord Derby had left. 'And I'm afraid most of your hair will have to go.'

Charles looked at his clothes. They were dirty and torn, but he knew George Penderel was right, they would tell his enemies that he was a Royalist nobleman. He then stroked his long black hair. It was dirty and greasy, but it would also help identify him. Charles immediately began to take off his clothes.

'Will, ask Mr Penderel, to give you a pair of scissors. You can have the honour.'

George Penderel found a pair of scissors and some woodsman's clothes made of coarse wool. Charles put on the clothes, covered his hands with soot from the chimney, and blackened his face. Then he sat down on a wooden stool and said to Will, 'Start cutting, lad.'

At first, Will only cut small bits off the ends, but Charles said, 'Don't worry, Will, I'm not going to send you to the Tower for this.'

Will took hold of the King's hair in one hand and placed the scissors high up near the neck. He closed his eyes and then snipped. He opened one eye and looked down at the floor where the hair had fallen. He snipped again, and again, gradually snipping faster. Soon, it was done. Will stood back and studied his work.

'Ugh!' he said, horrified 'You look awful!'

'Excellent,' said Charles, 'that means you've done a good job.' He stood up and clapped Will on the back. 'Well done, lad.'

But the main problem was shoes. Charles had such large feet that George Penderel could not find a pair to fit. The best he could find were about three sizes too small. Charles squeezed into them, but he knew that it would make walking to London very painful.

After drinking a glass of sack each and nibbling a biscuit, Charles and Will followed George Penderel out of the back door. It had been decided that it was too dangerous for the King to stay in the house all day.

It was a dull September morning. The smell of rain was in the air. Carrying a billhook to complete his disguise, Charles looked like a real peasant. He made Will laugh by speaking to him in a countryman's accent.

They soon reached a wood called Spring Coppice. Will thought how beautiful it looked, with all the leaves turning crimson and gold. He remembered other autumn days, when he and his father had walked in their local wood, hunting for rabbits.

Light rain now began to fall so George Penderel stopped under a large beech tree. He laid down a woollen blanket for the King and Will to sit on.

'I'll come for Your Majesty this evening just before sunset. I would advise you not to move about much, just in case Roundhead patrols decide to search the wood.'

Charles thanked George Penderel, and he and Will sat down with their backs against the trunk of the beech tree.

The rain continued to fall.

CHAPTER THREE

'Do you realise,' said the King, as rain dripped down through the branches of the beech tree and onto his woodsman's hat, 'I have not eaten a good meal for nearly two days. All I've had is a crust of bread, some biscuits, a mug of ale and a glass of sack. I'm starving!'

'Me and Dad...' Will stopped himself for a moment as the pain of his loss returned. He used his sleeve to wipe his eyes and then continued, 'We'd sometimes go without any food for days. We had to catch everything we ate.' Will looked at Charles. 'What would Your Majesty normally eat at one meal at court?'

The young King frowned for a moment and then broke out into a smile as he began to remember.

'Well, we'd start with the meat dishes first – venison, pork, lamb, pigeon, duck.'

'All at once!' said Will, gaping.

'Naturally,' said Charles. 'The sauces, of course, would be served on separate silver dishes, as would the vegetables. Then we would end with honey and almond cakes, cornflour pudding with jam, and sugared fruits. It would all be washed down with excellent wines. What I would give for some meat now...'

Suddenly Will said, 'I can hear something. It sounds like horses.'

Charles got to his feet and grabbed hold of the woollen blanket. 'Quick, we've got to find some cover.'

He and Will ran towards some bramble bushes. They dropped to their knees and pulled themselves into the heart of a bush. They scratched their faces and hands but they did not dare cry out.

Pointing, Will whispered, 'Look! Roundhead Cavalry!'

They watched a troop of about thirty horsemen ride past. Will and Charles were well hidden from view, but the sight of the horsemen made the King feel very uneasy.

Charles looked at Will. 'I bet the whole countryside is crawling with them,' he said, once the horsemen were out of sight. 'I don't think we'll make it on foot to London. And I don't think it's wise to go north to Scotland. That leaves Wales. There are plenty of Royalists there and we could make for Swansea, and try and take a boat to France.'

Will nodded.

When George Penderel came back in the late afternoon, Charles told him of his plan to make for Wales. They went back to Mr Penderel's house for something to eat – a plate of bacon and eggs each. Not a royal dish, but to Will it was a feast.

As the sun was setting, they set off across country. The rain had stopped, but the ground was very soggy, and this, together with the tight fitting shoes, made walking very difficult for Charles. Within minutes his feet began to hurt, as he trudged across muddy fields, squeezed through thorn hedges, and waded across deep, fast flowing streams.

After two hours, they came to a river. They found they could cross it by using a mill-bridge. George Penderel opened the gate to allow the King and Will through. On closing it, however, Mr Penderel let it snap back. Immediately, the front door of the mill house opened. A man appeared, dressed in a white nightshirt. He called out.

'Hey! You there. Stand still!'

'Good evening, sir!' said George Penderel, trying

to sound relaxed. 'Sorry if we've disturbed you. We are just on our way home.'

'Do you live around these parts?' said the man at the door.

'Yes, that's right,' answered George. 'I live about five miles to the west of the river. This man and boy are my servants.'

'I've never seen you before,' said the man.

'I have only been in the area for a couple of months.'

But the man was not happy. He turned his head and shouted inside. 'You men, come out here! We've got some suspicious looking characters hanging around.'

About five or six other men appeared at the door.

'I think they're soldiers,' Will whispered. 'We'd better make a run for it.'

'I reckon the lad might be right, Your Majesty,' said George.

The three turned back, ran across the bridge, and up the lane on the opposite side of the bridge. Behind them they heard shouts of 'Stop there! Stop, I say!' but they kept on running. It was very muddy because of the rain and Charles fell over a couple of times. Then, out of sight of the mill house and out of breath, they hid behind a hedge and waited for half an hour to make sure they were not followed.

Two hours later they arrived at the house of Mr Woolfe, who George Penderel knew was a Royalist. But on being woken in the middle of the night, Mr Woolfe was not too keen to help.

'Roundhead soldiers are all over the place. They're going around searching houses,' he said, sleepily, from his upstairs window. 'I'll not risk my neck unless it is the King himself you have with you.'

George Penderel said, 'It is the King I have with me.'

On hearing this, Mr Woolfe almost fell out of the window. He came down immediately and opened the front door. He sat the King in his comfiest chair and brought in some cold meat for everybody. Will helped Charles take off his shoes. He was shocked to see the King's swollen and bloody feet.

'It is impossible, Sire,' said Mr Woolfe, on hearing of the King's plans to cross the River Severn and go into Wales. 'All the bridges are guarded, and so too are the ferries. Your Majesty would certainly be caught.'

Charles looked at his poor feet and said, 'Then we must abandon our plans.'

Will looked up at the King, and for the first time since he had met him, he saw doubt in his eyes. Bathing the King's feet in a bowl of warm water, he said. 'Don't worry, Your Majesty, we'll make it. God is on your side.'

. . . . .

After hiding all day in Mr Woolfe's barn, Charles and Will returned to George Penderel's house. There, the King found Colonel Carlis in hiding. The Colonel, who had stayed at the battle of Worcester to see the last man fall, was one of Charles's most loyal and brave commanders.

The King and Will, together with Colonel Carlis, spent the rest of that day hiding in a huge oak tree on the estate. The tree was so tall, they had to climb into it by using a wooden ladder provided by

George Penderel. Will was impressed by how quickly the King climbed up into the branches. Charles laughed.

'When I was a lad I spent hours climbing trees.'

'You mean you played the same kind of games as peasant children?' said Will, amazed.

'Will,' said Charles, 'you will find very little difference between rich and poor boys.'

Will looked into the King's eyes, 'Except for hunger, Your Majesty.'

Once more, Will's honest answer made the young King feel uncomfortable. He put his hand on Will's shoulder.

'If I ever get to rule this land, Will, I promise you, you will never go hungry again.'

The top of the tree bushed out so much that they were completely hidden from view. They brought with them bread, cheese and beer, and a couple of cushions for Charles to lay his head against. He and Will had not slept for three days.

'Put one of these under your head, lad,' Charles said to Will, throwing him one of the cushions.

Will's eyes lit up. He had never slept on a real cushion before. He put it down across two broad branches and gently patted it. 'It's so soft!' he said.

The King had more difficulty in getting comfortable, so, in the end, Colonel Carlis put the cushions on his knees. Charles curled up in a ball and laid his head on the cushions. Both he and Will quickly dropped off to sleep.

It was the sound of hooves that woke Will with a start. For a moment, he had no idea where he was. Then he looked across and saw Colonel Carlis, who with one hand put a finger to his lips and then pointed down. Will nodded that he understood.

Horsemen had stopped right underneath their oak tree. One of them spoke.

'This is hopeless. He could be hiding anywhere.'

'Don't worry,' said another, 'the reward money will make someone talk. We'll catch him, you'll see. And when we do, he'll end up like his father, on the block!' The rest of the horsemen laughed.

The Colonel now pointed to his other arm which was wedged under the cushion and the King's head. The agony in the Colonel's face told Will that the arm had gone numb. Will realised they were in big trouble.

The Colonel tried to move his arm slowly but in doing so, it made Charles give out a loud moan.

'What was that?' said one of the horsemen.

'Sounds like it came from up above us,' said another, 'from inside the tree.'

'Right, Taylor. You're the youngest. Up you go and see if there's anyone hiding in there.'

Will Symons drew his knife and waited.

CHAPTER FOUR

Looking down through the turning leaves, Will could see the face of a young Roundhead soldier slowly getting closer to him. Will's throat felt very dry. He knew that in a few moments time he might have to kill the young soldier, who only looked about 16 years old. The same age, Will thought, as his brother Tom, when he was killed at the battle of Dunbar exactly a year ago.

Then, just as it seemed the young soldier, who was standing on a large man's shoulders, would pop his head through the canopy of leaves, there was a shout. The man at the bottom of the tree turned to listen and the young soldier lost his balance and went crashing to the ground. Will heard him moan and saw him struggle to his feet, holding his left shoulder. The rest of the soldiers laughed.

'I couldn't help it, Captain,' said the young Roundhead. 'It wasn't my fault. Reynolds moved and made me fall, and now I've hurt my shoulder!'

'Stop complaining, Taylor,' said his captain, 'and get back on your horse. We've just heard that some Cavaliers have been sighted only three miles away and we've been ordered to give chase.'

Will watched the young soldier struggle onto his horse and ride away. Silently, he wished him good luck.

Colonel Carlis now moved his arm from under the King's head and started to rub it to get the blood flowing again. This woke Charles from his deep sleep. He looked at the faces of his two friends.

'Ah, my good fellows,' said Charles. 'Have I missed anything since I dozed off?'

'Nothing that young Will here couldn't cope with, Your Majesty. I don't think you could have chosen a more brave and loyal companion.' The Colonel smiled at Will, who blushed.

. . . . .

As soon as it was dark the three fugitives returned to the Penderel's house for supper. While they ate some chicken, George Penderel told them that he had run into a large troop of Roundhead soldiers in the village that day.

'They are putting posters all over the place,' said

George. 'They are offering a reward of £1,000 for the capture of "Charles Stuart, a tall man upwards of two yards high".'

Will saw the young King's face suddenly turn very grim.

'That's a fortune,' said Charles. 'Surely it will tempt many poor people.'

'It won't be the poor who betray His Majesty,' said Will sharply. 'Not even for a hundred thousand pounds! The poor may have no money, but that won't turn them into traitors. My father said that the King of England belongs to all of us, poor and rich alike, and that he has been chosen by God. And no man has the right to challenge the will of God.'

Everyone in the room was moved by Will's speech.

'Your father was a remarkable man, Will,' said Charles. 'I'm sorry I never got to know him, but I am proud to count his son as my good friend. I no longer have any doubts.'

That night, after saying goodbye to Colonel Carlis, Charles and Will set off across country with George Penderel and his five brothers, together with the servant, Francis Yates. They were all armed with either a pitchfork or billhook. Charles wanted to find his friend, Lord Wilmot, and tell him of his plans. He was still dressed in his woodsman's clothes and rode with Will on a very large carthorse belonging to the Penderels.

'This is the heaviest beast I've ever ridden,' said the King, after riding for a couple of miles.

'A good thing it is heavy,' said George Penderel, 'for it is carrying the weight of three kingdoms on its back!'

They were making for Mosely Hall about 10 miles away. When they got near, the King and Will got off their carthorse to walk the rest of the way. All the others, except for George Penderel and Francis Yates, were sent back. Charles was so keen to get going, he forgot to thank the poor men who had risked their lives for him. He turned around and ran after them.

'I'm sorry,' he said, 'my troubles made me forget my manners. I thank you all.' Then he gave the men his hand to kiss.

Mosely Hall was owned by Mr Whitgreave, an ex-soldier and loyal Royalist. He had been hiding Lord Wilmot in a secret priest hole for several days. Now, he was nervously waiting in his orchard for the fugitives to arrive. As the party finally appeared, he immediately recognised George Penderel and Francis Yates, but not the dirty looking woodsman and young boy.

'Where is the King, Penderel?' said Mr Whitgreave, looking alarmed. 'Have you left him in the woods?'

'You don't have to worry, Mr Whitgreave, Sir,'

said Charles. He spoke in the accent of a poor countryman. 'He's not been left in the woods.'

'Then where is he, man?'

Charles straightened his back, lifted his head and took off his battered old hat. 'He stands before you.' he said in his normal voice.

Mr Whitgreave's jaw dropped. He fell onto his right knee. 'Your Majesty! Please forgive me, I did not recognise you!'

'Stand, Mr Whitgreave,' said Charles, secretly pleased that his disguise was so complete. 'It is I who should ask your forgiveness for playing my silly joke on you.'

'If it had not been God's will that his Majesty should sit on the English throne, then I feel sure he would make a fine career on the stage.' said Mr Whitgreave.

'Who knows?' said Charles, with a rye smile. 'If God has a sense of humour, it may be that it will be an actor's life for me.' He turned to Will. 'What do you think, lad? Would you fancy the idea of roaming the courts of Europe with me, entertaining Kings and Emperors?'

Will lifted a hand up in front of him, and began to walk up and down.

'"Is this a dagger which I see before me,
The handle toward my hand?
Come let me clutch thee."'

Charles laughed at the astonished faces of his two companions and Mr Whitgreave. 'Gentlemen, don't you recognise the work of Mr William Shakespeare, England's greatest playwright?'

'My father was a travelling player,' said Will. 'I'm named after Shakespeare. My family used to go to the fairs up and down the country and perform. Dad said that the closing of all the theatres by Oliver Cromwell was a wicked sin.'

'I promise you, young Will Symons,' said Charles, 'that if I regain my throne, one of the first things I'll do is re-open the theatres and you can perform for me at my court. And now Mr Whitgreave, shall we go into the house and eat? All this play acting as a woodsman has given me a King's appetite!'

At Moseley Hall Charles was re-united with his old friend, Lord Wilmot. Unlike the King, Wilmot had made no effort to disguise himself. When not hiding in the priest hole at the hall, he rode everywhere as if he was a country gentleman out for a Sunday picnic. He was shocked by his royal friend's appearance.

'You look absolutely awful,' he said to Charles as the King sat having his sore feet bathed by Will. 'It's undignified for the King of England to look like a peasant.'

'You're wrong, Wilmot. I am proud to wear these tattered clothes, for it is the peasants of this country who are risking their lives for me. It is a humbling experience; you ought to try it.'

'Bah!' said Wilmot, 'I'll continue living in gentleman's clothes, thank you very much.'

Charles laughed and then said, 'At least when you're caught by the Roundheads, My Lord, you will be shot like a gentleman.'

Later that evening, Mr Whitgreave showed Charles and Will the secret priest hole. They approached it through a bedroom. A secret door in one of the wood panels led them into another small bedroom. Then, a trap door in the floor of a cupboard revealed the secret hiding place. It was dark and airless, but there was enough room for the King to lie down in comfort. Little did he realise how important to his safety the priest hole would be.

The next two days passed pleasantly enough. Will spent time with Alice, the young kitchen maid. Like him, she was a Catholic and an orphan. Charles, meanwhile, together with Lord Wilmot and Mr Whitgreave, planned the next stage of the King's escape. Wilmot had met with a Colonel Lane, a Royalist soldier, who lived close to Moseley.

'Colonel Lane's younger sister, Jane,' said Wilmot, 'has been given a travel pass by the local Roundhead commander, for herself and her manservant, to travel down to Abbots Leigh near Bristol. A friend of her's is about to have a baby and she wants Jane to come and help out at the house. Your Majesty could travel with Jane as her manservant, then take a boat from Bristol to France.'

'Will must come too,' said Charles.

'But, the pass is only for one manservant. Why take the added risk, especially for a peasant boy?' said Wilmot.

'The lad has been a lucky mascot for me,' said Charles. 'And he is teaching me about my people. He comes with me. That's my final word. Besides, if we get stopped, we can say that we thought the pass was for any number of Jane's servants.'

'As Your Majesty wishes,' said Wilmot, 'but I don't like it.'

Later that afternoon, Charles felt sleepy and went to lie down on a bed. Lord Wilmot rode over to Colonel Lane's house to finalise the escape plans. Will was walking in the orchard with Alice.

'Will you go with the King to France?' Alice asked.

'If he wants me to. But if not, I could always stay with my Aunt Martha in Bristol.'

'What would you do at your Aunt's?'

'I don't know really,' said Will. 'I'd like to join another band of travelling players. Maybe, I'll come ...' Will stopped dead in mid sentence. He looked out across the rolling countryside.

'Oh, no!' he cried.

He spun round and, without a word of explanation to Alice, ran in the direction of the house. He dashed through the main entrance and up the staircase. Without knocking, he burst into the bedroom where the King was lying down. He pulled Charles up by an arm and dragged him to the window. As the King rubbed the sleep from his eyes, Will pointed.

'Your Majesty, Roundhead cavalry are heading straight for the house! They'll soon have the place surrounded!'

CHAPTER FIVE

Will fastened the trapdoor which led to the secret priest hole, then he ran downstairs. At the bottom, he was met by a worried Mr Whitgreave.

'I've made sure our friend is safe, Sir,' said Will.

Mr Whitgreave nodded. 'Good lad, Will. Now I want you to go and open all the doors of the house, including the back door. I'll go to the front and greet our visitors.'

Will did as he was asked. When he arrived at the kitchen, he found Alice and Mary, the cook, looking out of the window. Will went to the door, which led out to the orchard, and opened it.

'What's happening, Will?' asked Alice.

'Roundhead soldiers,' answered Will. 'Come to search the house I bet.'

'Looking for your Royalist Cavalier?' said Alice.

'I'm sure of it,' said Will.

Will felt a bit awkward. He had come to like Alice a lot in the last couple of days, but he had not told her that it was the King himself hiding in the house. No-one knew, except for Mr Whitgreave and Lord Wilmot.

He must be very important, then,' said Mary.

'All good servants of the King are important,' said Will. 'And His Majesty will not forget any of them when once again he sits on the throne.'

Loud and angry voices could now be heard coming from the front of the house. Will went to find out what was going on. To his horror, he saw

Mr Whitgreave, who was surrounded by soldiers, being struck across his face by the Roundhead commander.

Will ran over to Mr Whitgreave who had fallen to the floor under the force of the blow.

'You've got no right to treat this man so, he's done nothing wrong!' he shouted angrily.

Suddenly, Will felt his collar being grabbed by a large, powerful hand. 'Hold your tongue, boy!' a rough voice growled.

The commander gave Will a cold stare before addressing Mr Whitgreave again. 'Where's the traitor, Charles Stuart?'

'I've no idea,' said Mr Whitgreave, 'maybe he has escaped to Holland.'

The commander grabbed Mr Whitgreave by his throat. 'We know that the Knave has been here.'

'If he was,' said Mr Whitgreave, 'he isn't here now. Search the house if you like. I've got nothing to hide.'

One by one soldiers appeared at the front of the house and shook their heads at their commander. Will could see that Mr Whitgreave's coolness was annoying him.

'I've got orders to arrest all Royalist officers who

fought at Worcester. So you'll have to come along with us.'

'Mr Whitgreave wasn't at Worcester,' shouted Will. 'He was sick in bed at the time.'

'Do you expect me to believe that, boy?'

'Ask his neighbours, here,' said Will.

A number of people had come up from the village to see what all the noise was about. Much to the Roundhead commander's annoyance, they said that Will was telling the truth. Mr Whitgreave did not fight at Worcester.

The commander stared into the eyes of Mr Whitgreave. 'You've been lucky this time, but we'll be back.' He waved his arm at his men and they all mounted their horses and rode off. Mr Whitgreave did not move until he saw that the soldiers were well out of sight. Then he said to Will.

'How did you know that I missed the battle through illness?'

Will blushed. 'Alice told me,' he said. 'I hope I didn't speak out of turn.'

'Don't be silly, boy, you showed much courage in standing up to those ruffians. I can see now why the King insists you travel with him. Now come, let us go and give him the all clear.'

Two days later King Charles and Will were travelling south towards Bristol. With them was Jane Lane and her cousin Henry Lascelles. The young King was dressed as a yeoman's son. The simple grey cloth and cloak were a great improvement on the rags he had been wearing recently. And at last someone had found the right sized shoes for his poor feet. He was travelling under the name of Will Jackson, which amused young Will.

It had been decided that Lord Wilmot would travel separately and meet up with the King later. Will, in particular, thought this was a good idea, as Wilmot refused to disguise himself and so ran a greater risk of being recognised and caught.

Charles and Jane rode on one horse, the King in the saddle and the young woman riding behind, while Will rode bareback behind Henry Lascelles. Although the dangers were just as great as before, at least Charles and Will could now travel on the open road.

They had set off early in the morning and were making good progress, when around midday Charles said to Jane, 'I'm afraid our horse has thrown a shoe. We're going to have to stop at the blacksmith in the next village to get it sorted out.'

A few minutes later they rode into the village of Bromsgrove. So as to not attract attention, it was decided that the King himself should take the horse to be shod.

'But what do I say?' said Charles. 'I've never taken

a horse to the blacksmith. I've always had servants to do that for me. I'm a decent rider, if I say so myself, but I've never even saddled my own horse.'

'I'll come with you if you like,' said Will, 'but you'll have to do the talking. It wouldn't look right if I spoke.'

They entered the smithy. The place was warm and steamy. The blacksmith was hammering a shoe on his anvil. Charles explained his problem in a perfect yeoman's accent. Will thought that the King really would make an excellent actor.

'Is there any news from Worcester?' asked Charles while the blacksmith inspected the horse's hoof.

'I've not heard that that rogue Charles Stuart has been caught, if that's what you mean,' said the smith. 'Some others have been taken, but not him.'

'I think when they catch this fellow,' said Charles, 'they ought to hang him immediately for all the trouble he's caused to parliament.'

'Spoken like an honest man, sir,' said the smith.

When they got going again they soon ran into trouble of another kind. A troop of Roundhead soldiers had stopped a little further up the road. They were obviously resting their horses, as they were gathered in small groups by the road side, chatting.

'I think we should ride straight through them,' said Charles. 'If they see us turn around, they might become suspicious.'

But Henry Lascelles disagreed. 'I think we ought to take a small detour off the road.'

Charles thought it was not wise for him to argue with a gentleman on the open road and so they did as Lascelles suggested. They made a detour of about three or four miles before entering the town of Stratford upon Avon.

They now rode straight into the same troop of soldiers, only this time they were mounted and in the middle of the road.

'Well,' said the King, 'we've got no choice this time. We've just got to ride through them.'

As they approached, the soldiers parted to allow the travellers through. Charles, much to the horror of Henry Lascelles, even traded some 'Good afternoons'. Even when they had passed on Lascelles still looked very pale. Charles couldn't help teasing him. 'You don't look too well, Henry.'

They stayed that night at a pre arranged house in Long Marston and next day made good progress to Cirencester, where they stayed in an inn. By mid afternoon on the third day they had reached the outskirts of Bristol. But danger lay ahead of them. They had to travel through the centre of the city to reach the village of Abbots Leigh.

'I was in Bristol for six months during the war,' Charles told his companions, 'and although I was only fifteen at the time, there is the risk that I might be recognised.'

'As long as we keep our nerve and keep moving, we shouldn't attract attention,' said Jane.

But, once inside Bristol, Charles stopped to study the new defensive walls built since the Roundheads took the city and it was some time before his anxious companions persuaded him to move on. As they set off again, the King turned to Will.

'Doesn't your Aunt live here in Bristol?' Will nodded. 'Then, don't you think you should go to her? It was your father's last wish.'

Will thought for a moment before he answered.

'My father gave his life for you and your father. So did my brothers. They would want me to do my duty and that's what I'm going to do. Aunt Martha will understand.' He suddenly grinned. 'I'll write to her from France.'

CHAPTER SIX

They reached Abbots Leigh by late afternoon and went straight to a magnificent house. It was a huge, timber framed building, dating from the reign of Queen Elizabeth I and set in large gardens. Jane and her party were made very welcome.

Immediately Jane spoke to her friend, Ellen Norton, who was the lady of the house. 'My manservant, Will Jackson, is not feeling very well,' she said. 'Would you mind if he went straight to bed.'

'Of course not,' said Ellen. 'I'll have his dinner sent up to his room and I'll get Dr Gorge to have a look at him. The doctor is staying with us at the moment.'

Charles was shown to his room by John Pope, the butler. Will went with them and he saw that Pope kept staring at the King, as though he was trying to remember where he had seen the face before. Charles noticed it too.

'Do you think he recognises you?' said Will when the butler had left.

'I'm not sure,' said Charles. 'You'd best keep an eye on him Will.'

After dinner had been served, Will sneaked back up to the King's bedroom.

'What have you found out, Will?'

'That John Pope is a Royalist, although some of the other servants are for Cromwell. They spent most of their meal time in the kitchen arguing about you. I mean you the King, not you, Will Jackson.'

Charles laughed. 'The good doctor is also a loyal subject of mine. When he came to examine me he kept going on and on about the Royal cause. I lay in the candle's shadow, terrified that he would recognise me. Sometimes your friends can be more dangerous to you than your enemies. Any news of Wilmot yet?'

Will shook his head. 'Not yet.'

There was a quiet knock at the door, which then opened. It was John Pope. 'I've come to collect your tray Mr Jackson,' he said. He walked over to the bed and looked first at Will and then at Charles. He appeared very uncomfortable.

'I know who you are,' he said nervously. 'You're the King.' He dropped to his knees. 'My old master was one of your father's courtiers. I used to go with him to Richmond when you were a lad.' He saw Charles look across at Will. 'Don't be alarmed, I won't give you away. I fought in your father's army during the war. Anything I can do to help, you just let me know.'

'There is something you can do immediately,' said Charles. 'You can bring Lord Wilmot to me when he arrives. Would you recognise him?'

'That I would, Sire, but so would many another in this house. I'll saddle up at once and meet him on the road. Then I'll bring him up to you in secret.'

After meeting up with Lord Wilmot and taking him to Charles, John Pope rode into the city of Bristol to see whether he could find a ship to take the King to France.

'There is not a ship available for at least a month, Sire,' said Pope on his return.

Charles was very disappointed. 'Then where do we go from here?' he said.

'I know of a safe house in the village of Trent, about forty miles from Abbots Leigh,' said Pope. 'From there, Your Majesty could make his escape from several channel ports. The owner of the house is a Colonel Wyndham.'

'I know Francis Wyndham well,' said Charles, smiling. 'He's a fine soldier.'

It was agreed that Lord Wilmot should go on ahead. Will was glad about this. He always felt nervous when Wilmot travelled with them. Charles, Will, Lady Jane and Lascelles were to follow a day later.

There were tears in Colonel Wyndham's eyes as he welcomed Charles to his house. 'I heard that Your Majesty had been killed at Worcester,' he said.

The Colonel had arranged for a Captain Ellesdon to provide a ship to sail from Charnmouth on the south coast. 'I told him the ship is for two royalist cavaliers on the run, and I've agreed a price of £60, to be paid when his man, a Captain Limbry, returns from France after making sure of Your Majesty's escape.'

At sunset a few days later Charles, Will, Lord Wilmot and Colonel Wyndham arrived at the village of Charnmouth and booked into one of the local inns. Lady Jane and Lascelles had returned home. As midnight approached, the four of them made their way down to the shore. All was quiet, except for a light wind blowing and the breakers crashing onto the steep shingle beach. All they could do was sit and wait. But minutes turned to hours, and Captain Limbry still did not arrive.

'I don't like it,' said Will. 'Something's gone wrong. I think we ought to get off the beach.'

'I think the lad is right,' said Colonel Wyndham. 'If soldiers arrive now, Your Majesty will be trapped.'

'But we don't know that the ship still won't appear,' said Wilmot. 'I think we should stay a bit longer.'

It was now getting light. They had to decide what they were going to do. Had Captain Limbry been taken by Roundhead soldiers or had he betrayed the King for the £1,000 reward?

In fact, Captain Limbry had been locked in his bedroom by his wife! She did not want him to go off on another trip so soon after coming back from his last one. But of course, Charles and his friends had no way of knowing this.

'I suggest,' said Colonel Wyndham,'that His Majesty, young Will and myself ride out along the London Road as far as Bridport, and wait in the best inn there, while Wilmot finds out what has gone wrong. If there has just been a mix up, we are close enough to the coast to try again, but if we've been betrayed, we can get the King away to safety.'

Wilmot agreed to this, and so they all went back to the inn to get their horses.

By midday, Charles, Will and Colonel Wyndham were approaching the town of Bridport. They saw that the place was swarming with Roundhead soldiers, who were getting ready to board ships to the island of Jersey, which was still holding out for the King.

'I don't think we should go into the town,' said Colonel Wyndham, a little nervously.

'But we must,' said Charles. 'We have agreed to meet Wilmot there. Besides, being on the run these weeks has taught me that one must be bold in these situations. What do you think, Will?'

'Having Lord Wilmot roaming the countryside in search of us is more worrying to me than a regiment of Roundhead soldiers.'

Will's comment even made the doubting Colonel laugh. 'I take your point, lad!'

Charles led Will and the Colonel straight into the centre of the town and up to the best inn. The yard was packed with soldiers. The King signalled to the others to dismount and he led them straight through the middle of the soldiers towards the stable. Some of them got very angry with him.

'Oy! You blundering oaf!,' shouted one, whom Charles had brushed aside. 'Watch what you're doing.'

'Well, get out of the way, then,' said Charles, pretending to be annoyed, 'or I'll report your rudeness to your company commander!'

Will saw poor Colonel Wyndham's face go white. He knew that the King was really enjoying himself.

Once inside the stable, the elderly hostler gave Charles a strange look.

'Don't I know your face?' he said, suspiciously.

'That depends,' said Charles cooly, 'on where you have lived.'

'I used to be ostler at Mr Potter's inn near Exeter.'

The King now remembered that he had stayed at Mr Potter's inn during the war. 'Oh,' said Charles, 'that's where you've seen me then. I worked for over a year at Mr Potter's when I was a lad. Well, you must excuse me, I must go and tend my master.'

As they left to go into the inn Will grinned. 'You're

getting good at this,' he said. 'You'll make a decent peasant after all.'

Later, in the evening, Lord Wilmot arrived at the inn. He had talked to Captain Ellesdon, who claimed he did not know why the ship had not turned up.

'What do we do now then?' said Will. 'I don't think we can risk going back to Charnmouth.'

'I suggest His Majesty returns to my house at Trent, until another ship can be found,' said Colonel Wyndham.

So next morning, the King set off to return to Trent. He was not to know that he had been recognised at Charnmouth, and that only a few minutes after he left Bridport, a company of Roundhead soldiers rode into the town to arrest him.

CHAPTER SEVEN

The King and Will spent nineteen frustrating days at Trent before another ship could be found to take them to France. But finally, after almost six weeks on the run, it seemed that escape was at hand.

They rode with Lord Wilmot to the tiny village of Brighton and took rooms at the George Inn. There Charles was introduced to the man who he hoped would take him to safety. His name was Nicholas Tettersell and he immediately recognised the King.

When Charles retired into another room, Tettersell said to Wilmot, angrily. 'I was told I was taking two business gentlemen across the Channel. It seems to me that £60 isn't much of a sum for transporting the King of England who has a price of £1,000 on his head.'

'I recognised him at once,' continued Tettersell. 'During the war, His Majesty captured my ship, 'The Surprise', just off the coast here. It was His

Majesty himself who released me and gave my ship back to me.'

Will, who was listening, knew they were in big trouble. What if Tettersell decided to turn them in for the reward? Wilmot must strike up a new deal with the man, or else they would have to kill him. Will touched the handle of his dagger.

There was an uneasy silence, then Wilmot said, 'In that case,Tettersell, you will know what a noble heart the King has. He gave you your freedom, now it is your turn to give the King his. I tell you what,' he continued, 'I will increase your payment to £200. You will receive this once the King has safely reached France. Do you agree?'

Mr Tettersell hesitated. Will hardly dared to breathe. Then at last, Tettersell spat on his hand and held it out to Lord Wilmot. 'Agreed.' The two men shook hands. Will smiled as Wilmot then wiped his hand on his tunic. He was not used to touching the hands of the lower classes.

Charles, Will and Wilmot boarded 'The Surprise' during the early hours of the morning. The ship would sail with the tide a few hours later.

'Are you sure you want to come with me, Will?' said Charles as the two of them stood on the deck. 'You are looking very serious.'

'I was just thinking about the last few months,' said Will. 'And about my father.'

'He would be very proud of you,' said Charles, 'just as I am. You have taught me more in the last six weeks about my people, than anyone else has done during my twenty one years on this earth. And if one day, God willing, I return to this land as its King, I shall not forget what the poor did for me in my hour of peril.'

Charles looked at Will gazing back at the beach.

'It seems that all those I love are always taken away from me,' said Will. 'There's no one left now except Aunt Martha.'

'Do you want to go to her?' asked Charles, gently.

'But I promised to go to France with you,' said Will.

'Then I release you from that promise. You have done your duty, Will Symons. Go to your Aunt and do so with my blessing.' He held out his arms to Will and hugged him.

Will struggled to hold back his tears. 'Shall I ever see you again?' he said.

'Of course you will. And when I do return, you can perform for me at my court with your travelling players. That is a royal command. Now off you go. You have a long way to travel.' The King put a purse of money in Will's hands. 'Get the landlord of the George to sell you a horse.'

Will touched his heart with his hand. 'You'll always be there,' he said.

Will Symons stood on the beach in the early morning light and watched as 'The Surprise' faded into the distance. He then turned and walked back into the village of Brighton. As he sat eating a breakfast of ham and eggs at the George Inn, the door burst open and a Roundhead captain walked in.

Will smiled to himself as he heard the captain declare, 'Landlord, I have reason to believe that a tall, dark man above two yards high is lodging here. He is the traitor Charles Stuart and I have a warrant here for his arrest.'

EPILOGUE

Oliver Cromwell died on 3 September 1658.

On 29 May 1660, Charles Stuart returned to London, nine years after his dramatic escape from the battle of Worcester, to a glorious reception. Thousands lined the streets to cheer his arrival into the city. It was also his thirtieth birthday. Immediately after his coronation, he set about rewarding those subjects who had risked their lives for him when he was on the run, especially the poor.

PLACES TO VISIT

Moseley Old Hall
Wolverhampton, Staffordshire (0902 782808). Charles II found refuge in this seventeenth century house, a National Trust property

The Commandery Museum
Worcester (0905 355071)

Upton House
Banbury, Oxfordshire (0295 670266). National Trust property near the Battle of Edgehill which was occupied at the time of the battle

Farnborough Hall
Banbury, Oxfordshire (0295 89202). National Trust property near the Battle of Edgehill which was occupied at the time of the battle

Edgehill Battle Museum
Banbury, Oxfordshire (0295 89593). This museum is in the estate of Farnborough Hall

Boscobel House
Shropshire, now an English Heritage property.

Civil War Walk
A guided walk around the city of Worcester

The Tower of London
Arms used in the Civil War

Oxburgh Hall
Norfolk. Collection of arms and armour from the time of the Civil War